The 10 Commandments of Strategic Networking

How To 'Up Your Networking Game' With Career and Business-Building Results!

Robert Bagley

Foreword By Caleb Paull

10 Commandments of Strategic Networking: How To 'Up Your Networking Game' With Career and Business-Building Results
Copyright © 2024 by Robert Bagley

ISBN: 979-8-8691-7941-8

LOC: 2024931764

Co-Pilot Publishing, 2024

Dedication

This book is dedicated to my wife, Larisa, and
my two daughters FaithAnn and Amanda.
They are what drive me to excel in
life and in my career every day.
I appreciate their sacrifice of time with me,
allowing me to be a networker (and author),
as it takes nights and sometimes weekends to
invest ample time into networking.
My wife has also accompanied me to
networking events, countless times, and for
that I am very appreciative.

Table of Contents

Foreword

You've heard it said that "it's not about what you know, but who you know". My personal experiences have led me to believe that it is not just who *you know*, but who *knows you*. When it's all said and done, you "knowing" people only gets you so far. What gets you exponentially further is other people knowing, trusting, remembering, and looking to you. Looking to you as an expert in your field, a reputable brand, a referral partner, a connector, and ultimately as a professional *resource*. One of the methods you should use to open the door for opportunities to "become known" and for the cultivation of professional relationships is networking.

One of the problems with networking is that many people do not understand what it is to begin with. And the challenge many people have with networking is they are not quite sure how to do it consistently, effectively, strategically, and professionally. I am confident that this book will act as a guide and bring about the concepts and clarity on how to approach networking properly and practically.

My perspective and position on this topic has grown by hosting *and* attending dozens of networking events, 10,000+ logged sales calls, and hundreds of 1-to-1 meetings.

After living in 4 states by the age of 23, I moved to Orlando Florida in January of 2020 with the intention of creating stability, establishing roots, and cultivating community. That desire came to an unexpected halt in March of 2020 when covid took control of society. Being in a brand-new city with a brand-new sales career in a field I knew nothing about did not pair well with a global societal shutdown. Amidst the challenges of social distancing and social uncertainty, I attempted to be outside more and meet my clients and prospects face-to-face as opposed to over the phone.

What most people do not see *now* is that my first time going outside for prospecting I was terrified. Who should I talk to? What should I say? What if they say no? What if they have a question that I don't have the answer to? My first in-person cold call I remember contacting my sales manager for reassurance before walking into the building to prospect.

What I later learned is that if you put yourself out there enough times, you *will* win. Over time, this principle translated into my networking efforts and has been refining me and my relationships ever since.

What I have come to understand over time is that they are people just like me and should be treated as such. We *must* learn to be more genuine both in our questions and in our responses during professional conversation. It is typically only when you put on the "salesman hat" of scripts and superficiality that you breed resistance and irritation.

Whether you've been networking for years, or have just begun, you know that a typical networking event is laced with the passing out of business cards, insincere questions about "what you do", scripted responses, and only a resilient few that follow up and follow *through* with what they say they will do.

It is up to *you* whether you will be one of those resilient few.

Many will claim that "the fortune is in the follow-up". While there is truth to that statement, I have come to discover that true and *lasting* fortune is found in the immediate, thoughtful, and consistent follow up. Follow-up is pointless in the absence of value, authenticity, and intentionality.

With that, I am honored for the opportunity to learn from Robert, who brings a genuine and practical approach to these "networking commandments". And for those who have spent any length of time with him know that he practices what he preaches, always. From our first conversation I have seen him navigate through a new city with great intention and personality. This has led him to great success in being seen, and more importantly, being *remembered*.

I pray that you will be enlightened, empowered, and equipped to master these 10 commandments of strategic networking. And that it will ultimately lead to more fruitful and significant relationships both in life and in business.

A fellow networker,

Caleb Paull
Founder and CEO of The VIP Co.

LinkedIn:
https://www.linkedin.com/in/the1calebpaull/
IG: https://www.instagram.com/the1calebpaull/
FB: https://www.facebook.com/the1calebpaull/

Preface

First, thank you for investing in yourself and this content.

Much admiration comes your way because you are seeking improvement personally and professionally. It is the hope of this author that you take away something (or several things) that will empower you to increase and improve-upon your skill and confidence level when it comes to your networking strategy and journey. Introducing…

"The 10 Commandments of Strategic Networking.
How To 'Up Your Networking Game' With Career and Business-Building Results!"

Whether you've never networked before, you just started networking, or you are a seasoned networking pro (if such a creature even exists), there will be many opportunities to take you to the next level in the "art" and sometime "science" of networking in this book.

<u>Writing Style of This Mini-Book</u>:
To keep in the spirit of a mini-book, this is written in conversational language and therefore the writing style will parallel this spirit. This means that I will use <u>underlines</u>, "quotes", ellipses (that's the 3 dots […]), lists, bullets, **bolds**, and dashes (-) to help your eyes and mind flow easily through the material.

Author's Note: Your middle school English teacher would most certainly NOT approve of my sentence structure and use of unorthodox use of punctuation, so we'll just keep it between us.

While I picked "Ten Commandments" of networking for the sake of keeping this content quickly-digestible and "mini" – there are certainly many other tips and recommendations that could lend to this discussion.

I would venture to say, arguably, that most of the other tips and recommendations not in this mini book would or could possibly fall into one these 10 "buckets."

These are "Commandments" for a reason as they are not merely "suggestions" because if you don't do these or ignore some (or all) of them, then your approach to networking will have less power and impact.

I can make these bold claims because I am a networker that's been "tried-in-the-fire" for decades and when I skip or ignore any of these, I inevitably pay the price somehow.

About The Author:

After I graduated from Bowling Green State University of Ohio with a Bachelor's Degree in Interpersonal and Public Communications, I started a carpet cleaning business in my early 20's with a pickup truck and a portable hot water extraction machine. I built that business up to having 5 trucks on the road (3 of them with truck-mounted hot water extraction machines) and 15 employees.

When I was 28 years old, I sold that business to a Paul Davis Systems Water and Fire Restoration Franchise. I had developed a turnkey, sellable business that was attractive to buy due to the systems I had put in place to run the business.

After I sold this business, I went to work for the carpet and flooring manufacturers in Sales. This included DuPont, Shaw, Mohawk, Beaulieu, and HMTX. My career took me from New York to San Francisco and Las Vegas, to Atlanta to Orlando (as I write this) and all points in between as at one point I covered the whole country when I lived in Atlanta.

Additionally, I've conducted Sales Training throughout the world; in the US, Canada, and even Israel and made it to the current position I hold as an Executive Vice President of Sales, where I now hire, coach, and manage Sale Professionals. At one point over 75 sales reps and their managers reported to me when I was an SVP at Beaulieu.

Each level has required me to become more skilled and MUCH MORE strategic in my business and professional networking activities.

Side Note: During my 10-year stint at Shaw Industries, a Berkshire Hathaway Company, I went back to school, this time grad school, and pursued my passion as a Theologian. Receiving my Masters of Theology from Northeastern Seminary in Rochester, NY – on the campus of Roberts Wesleyan College. This is how I got into publishing.

During my time as a Seminarian, I went to one of my professor's office hours and told him I wanted to write books. He said, "writing is overrated and hard work and no fun at all!" Wow, now those words of "encouragement" were all I needed to pique my curiosity about writing even more!

However, he was right about most of what he said, except the part that writing is overrated. I proved him wrong because now that I have a number one ranked publication day in and day out, therefore I can't subscribe to that piece of his negativity toward writing.

Writing IS hard, it is not for everyone, that's why not everyone does it, even though everyone during their adult life says, "I should write a book on that…"

Ultimately, my suggestion to business professionals of all levels is that everyone should write a book or at least an article or blog at some point in their business career.

I will say it is fun once you start writing and get a flow, kind of like this last paragraph, but no one wants to stop the busy pace of "do, do, do, scroll, scroll, scroll" to sit quietly (with no distractions) and think/articulate one's thoughts in writing.

It requires one to be diligent, intentional, and a little introverted to pull it off!

Subsequently, throughout my various Sales, Business Development, and Leadership roles, I had to "up-my-game" as a Networker by joining, attending, and participating in…

- Trade Association Events

- Non-profit Outreaches such as Habitat for Humanity, Salvation Army, Toys 4 Tots, Make-a-Wish, etc.
- Local networking events such as Chambers of Commerce and Political Events (I even ran for Mayor of my current City)
- Trade Shows – small city shows as well as big city shows in Vegas, New York, Dallas, Toronto, San Fran, LA, etc.
- Private Business Clubs
- Joining various committees of many of these organizations
- And many more, but those are the major highlights.

Some networking events where I "practiced my craft" ranged in size from several people to 800+ people at a San Francisco Trade Association Breakfast. From small, local trade shows in Upstate New York to Huge Trade shows in LA, Chicago, Vegas, Dallas, and New York City where tens of thousands of attendees swarmed the halls and booths!

Consequently, I've been networking for two and a half decades now and while I will never say, "I've arrived" ... I can certainly help you shorten your learning curve and save you from all the mistakes I've made over the years. I feel as though if you named something that could go wrong in networking, I've probably done it!

By reading this book, I guarantee if you just put these Commandments into practice, you will thank me later when you are spared embarrassment, fear, and God-forbid… head/heart-aches, and lost sleep.

Sparing you from these calamities will be your reward for consuming this content and then putting it into practice!

<u>For more information you can follow me at these various links below</u>:
- ➢ To track my current and on-going Networking activities and "nuggets of truth" follow me on my LinkedIn page at…
  <u>https://www.linkedin.com/in/robertbagley3rd</u>

- ➢ View my Professional Profile Website at…
  <u>http://robertbagley3rd.com</u>

- ➢ To enjoy a Podcast where I discuss my experiences and dive more into networking strategies, please visit this interview of me with Luminary Panel hosts, Chonsten Jennings and Lilliana Fedewa at…
  "How To Overcome Setbacks to Keep Succeeding No Matter What!"
  <u>https://youtu.be/x2vjb-yTon8?si=ajWFD_G0EMiuJ52o</u>

- ➢ To see my other "mini-books" and published work, please visit my Author Page at…
  <u>https://amazon.com/author/rb3</u>

One more Encouraging Note from the Author

*"It's never simply about getting what you want."
touts Keith Ferrazzi, "It's about getting what you
want and making sure that the people who are
important to you get what they want, too."*

Keith Ferrazzi and Tahl Raz, *"Never Eat Alone and Other
Secrets To Success, One Relationship At A Time."* 2005, Crown
Publishing Group, inside sleeve.

Networking is a valuable skill that can help you establish connections, build relationships, and open doors to new opportunities. While cold-calling, email and social media marketing, and lead generation of all kinds will always be important tools to gain more business, networking has a very important role to play in one's career for numerous reasons which will be highlighted throughout this mini-book.

These strategies outlined in this work will serve as your personal mindset coach. I say this because at the heart of anything in life or business, your positive mindset and attitude (regardless of your circumstances) will be the most important part of anything you seek to master, most especially your networking journey.

Here Are The "10 Commandments of Networking" Summary List…

Thou Shall:

1. Define Your Goals

2. Attend Industry Events

3. Be Approachable and Friendly

4. Be Elevator Speech Ready, ALWAYS!

5. Build A Diverse Network

6. Follow Up!

7. Utilize Social Media

8. Offer Value

9. Attend Informal Gatherings

10. Maintain Relationships

Now we will endeavor to "right-click" on each of these to round-out the mini-book:

<u>Commandment 1</u>

1. Define Your Goals:

Determine what you hope to achieve through networking. It always helps to write down your goals as it solidifies, in a material and meta-physical way, your mental ascent. Some questions you could ask yourself as you define and refine your networking goals can be centered around…

Are you looking for…
➢ Job Opportunities?
➢ Mentorship Relationships?
➢ Industry Knowledge or Partnerships?
➢ Career Advancement/Promotion
➢ All (or some) of the Above?
➢ Something Else?

Clarifying your goals will help you focus your efforts and make meaningful connections.

The Goals of a Business Networker

As a mindset coach, I believe the most important goal of a business networker is to build relationships. When you network with others, you are not just trying to sell them your product or service, you are trying to get to know them, understand their needs, and see how you can help them.

When you build relationships with other business professionals, you create a network of people who can support you in your career.

They can refer new clients and meaningful connections to you, give you advice and feedback, and help you find new opportunities.

Here are some of the specific <u>goals</u> that a business networker should have:

- <u>Meet new people.</u> The more people you meet, the larger your network will be. This means you will have more opportunities to generate leads, find new clients, and build relationships with potential partners. I look at networking as a large jigsaw puzzle and every networking event you attend gives you an opportunity to gain another piece of the puzzle. This helps you get closer to your destiny, purpose, and to meet the next new person that accelerates you toward that end.
- <u>Learn about other businesses</u>. When you network with other business professionals, you can learn about their industries, products, and services. This knowledge can help you stay ahead of the curve and make informed decisions about your own business.
- <u>Get referrals.</u> One of the best ways to get new clients and meaningful connections is through referrals. When you network with other business professionals, you can ask them to refer you to their customers, colleagues, and friends.
- <u>Find new opportunities.</u> Networking can help you find new job opportunities, partnership opportunities, and investment opportunities. When you meet new people, let them know what you are looking for and they may be able to help you find it.

To be a successful business networker, it is important to have a positive attitude and a genuine interest in getting to know other people. You should also be prepared to give back to your network. Offer your help and support to others, and they will be more likely to return the favor.

I encourage you to think of networking as a tool in your arsenal to build relationships and create a community of support. When you approach networking with this mindset, you will be more likely to achieve your goals.

Here are some additional <u>tips</u> for being a successful business networker:

- <u>Be prepared.</u> Before you attend a networking event, take some time to research the other attendees and identify the people you want to meet.
- <u>Be genuine.</u> People can tell when you are being fake, so be yourself and let your personality shine through.
- <u>Be a good listener.</u> People appreciate it when you take the time to listen to what they have to say. Ask questions and show that you are interested in learning more about their business. Try not to let your eyes wander away from the people you are speaking with. This is hard because you are always wanting to see who else is in the room you need to speak with.
- <u>Be helpful.</u> Offer your help and support to others, even if it is something small like introducing them to someone else or sharing a helpful article.

- <u>Follow up.</u> This is so important, it's one of the 10 Commandments (#6) on its own, but worth repeating throughout – and I will.

  Therefore, after you meet someone at a networking event, send them a follow-up email or connect with them on LinkedIn – or both. This will help you stay in touch and build relationships.

<u>Personal Example</u>:

I have a saying about networking that goes something like this, "Connect someone you just met with someone that can directly or indirectly help them and you have now endeared yourself to your new connection." I met a President of a large Janitorial Firm at a networking event, and I asked him, "How can I be of help to you?" at the end of our conversation and he said, "I need people, good people, to work for our company." "Say no more," I told him, tomorrow in your email box I will make an introduction to account manager at a phenomenal staffing firm that I had met a few weeks ago at a (of course) a networking event. I did what I said I would do and the two of them connected the very next day so he could tell the staffing firm his needs. The President of this Janitorial firm is now a very close connection of mine…and so is the staffing firm!

Commandment 2

2. Attend Industry Events:

Attend conferences, seminars, trade shows, and other events related to your field of interest. These gatherings offer excellent networking opportunities, allowing you to meet professionals, exchange ideas, and stay updated on industry trends.

Attending industry events is an essential part of being a successful business networker. Industry events provide you with the opportunity to meet new people, learn about the latest trends in your field, and build relationships with potential clients, partners, and mentors.

Here's a deeper dive on some of the key benefits of attending industry events:

- Meet new people. Industry events attract people from all over your industry, from entry-level employees to CEOs. This is a great opportunity to meet new people and expand your professional network.
- Learn about the latest trends. Industry events often feature keynote speakers, expert panels, and workshops on the latest trends and developments in your field. This is a great way to stay ahead of the curve and learn new things that can help you grow your business.
- Build relationships. Industry events provide you with the opportunity to build relationships with potential clients, partners, and mentors. By attending industry events and getting to know

people, you can create a network of people who can support you in your career.

Here are some <u>tips</u> for making the most of your time at industry events:

- <u>Have a game plan.</u> Before you attend an industry event take some time to research the other attendees and identify the people you want to meet. You may have to ask the event host for this list if it's not viewable online or in a viewable registry. By doing this research and due diligence before the event, you will make the most of your time and ensure that you don't miss out on any opportunities.
- <u>Be prepared to introduce yourself.</u> When you meet someone new at an industry event, be prepared to introduce yourself and your business concisely. Make sure to highlight your unique value proposition and what you can offer to the other person.
- <u>Be engaged</u> by asking questions and show that you are interested in learning more about them and their business.
- <u>Follow up</u> – here it is again! After you meet someone at an industry event, send them a handwritten note or a follow-up email or connect with them on social media. This will help you stay in touch and further build the relationship.

In conclusion, attending industry events is a great way to grow your business and achieve your career goals. By following the tips above, you can make the most of your time at industry events and build a network of relationships that will benefit you for years to come.

Personal Example:

When I was a Shaw Commercial Carpet Tile Sales Rep, I had taken on a new territory that was doing $400,000 in sales from Pittsburgh, PA to Albany, NY. Within 18 months, I had that thing humming to $1.4 million in sales! I had asked my previous boss if I could attend the iconic trade show in the Commercial Interiors space called *NeoCon* in Downtown Chicago. He told me I could go, but later rescinded the offer for reasons unknown to this day. So, taken back by this, I said, "I'll tell you what, I'll take several vacation days, fly myself out to Chicago for the show and pay all my own expenses if you will just let me work our product booth." He said I could do that. When I arrived, I worked that booth like CRAZY! I greeted as many people that came in as possible, took them around the showroom booth, told them all about our products, and <u>WORKED</u> <u>MY</u> <u>CAN</u> <u>OFF</u>! At the end of the show, my boss said, "Don't think that what you did went unnoticed, Management saw and was very impressed! Submit all your expenses for reimbursement and I have six months to promote you." Well, six months later, almost to the day, I was promoted! Which landed me a Regional Vice President's role and an executive relocation package that moved us from Rochester,

NY to San Francisco! This, and many other stories, I have highlighted the power of career-building opportunities I've uncovered at Industry Trade Events.

As a sales coach and trainer, I encourage you to think of attending industry events as an opportunity to learn, grow, and network!
Don't be afraid to step outside of your comfort zone and meet new people.
You never know who you might meet or what opportunities might come your way.

Commandment 3

3. Be Approachable and Friendly:

Approach networking with a positive attitude. Smile, make eye contact, and show genuine interest in others. Be open to conversation and make an effort to listen to others intently during your engagements.

Being approachable and friendly can help you make a memorable impression and is one of the most important qualities of a successful business networker. When you are approachable and friendly, people are more likely to want to talk to you and get to know you. This makes it easier for you to build relationships, which is essential for networking success.

Let's look a little closer at the <u>benefits</u> of being approachable and friendly as a Business Networker:

- <u>People are more likely to talk to you.</u> When you are approachable and friendly people feel more comfortable coming up to you and starting a conversation. This gives you more opportunities to meet new people and expand your network.
- <u>People are more likely to remember you.</u> When you make a positive impression on someone, they are more likely to remember you. This is important because people are more likely to do business with people they know and like.
- <u>People are more likely to trust you.</u> This is important because trust is essential for building strong relationships.

Here are a few more <u>tips</u> on how to be approachable and friendly:

- <u>Smile</u>. A smile is one of the simplest and most effective ways to make yourself more approachable. When you smile, you show people that you are friendly and open to talking. Also, accompany your smile with tools like mints and a toothpick to ensure a fresh, clean smile.
- <u>Firm handshake</u>. Don't have a limp, dead fish handshake, make it a firm grip as it shows confidence and intentionality.
- <u>Make eye contact</u> – yes, this keeps popping up, but always worth repeating at any juncture. Eye contact shows people that you are interested in them and what they have to say. It also helps to build rapport.
- <u>Be yourself and let your personality shine through.</u> People can tell when you are being fake, so it is important to be genuine.
- <u>Offer your help and support to others</u>, even if it is something small. This shows that you are a caring and supportive person. Remember, everyone's favorite radio station is WIIFM (What's In It For Me).
- **<u>Dress for success!</u>** I always strive to be the best dressed man in the room. When you do this, it shows that you care, and you set the tone of the room when you walk in. I call this,

"Being the Thermostat
and
Not the Thermometer."

This is a personal brand-builder fundamental that cannot be over emphasized. It's also the law of attraction that will super-charge your approachability.

In summary, being approachable and friendly is one of the most important things you can do as a business networker. By following these tips, you can make yourself more approachable and build stronger relationships with other business professionals.

I encourage you to think of being approachable and friendly as a sure proof way attract positive energy and opportunities into your life. When you put out good energy, you will get it back in return.

<u>Personal Example:</u>

After a networking event in Orlando, a young gentleman I had never met came up to me and said, "When I saw you during the event, I knew I needed to come up and meet you!" He complimented my attire and demeanor, and he ended up being a great photographer who I subsequently hired to do some work for my business and my personal brand.
You never know who you will attract…
BE A MAGNET!

Commandment 4

4. Be Elevator Speech Ready, ALWAYS!

Prepare (and always be ready to deliver) a concise and compelling elevator speech that introduces yourself and highlights what you do.

This brief self-introduction can be shared during public introductions at networking events or when meeting someone new one-on-one. Practice your pitch to ensure it sounds natural and engaging.

An elevator speech is a brief, persuasive statement that summarizes what you do and what makes you unique. It should be no more than 30-60 seconds long, so that you can deliver it in the time it takes to ride an elevator.

An elevator speech is an essential tool for Business Networkers. It allows you to introduce yourself quickly and easily to others and explain who you are and your profession. It is also a great way to make a positive first impression and generate interest in you and your business.

Here are some of the <u>benefits</u> of having an elevator speech as a business networker:

- <u>Introduce yourself quickly and easily.</u> When you have a well-crafted elevator speech, you can introduce yourself to others smoothly without having to fumble for words. This is especially important at Networking events where you may only have a few seconds to make a good impression.

- It allows you to explain what you do clearly and concisely. This will help others to understand your business and how you can help them or how they can best help you. I always like to tell people what a good customer is for me. Example: at the end of my elevator speech I sometimes say, "…and a good customer for me is Government Contractors, Hotels, and Hospitals."
- A concise elevator speech generates interest in your business. This means that it should highlight your unique value proposition and what you can offer to others.

Tips for crafting an effective elevator speech:
- Start with a strong opening. Your opening statement should grab the listener's attention and make them want to learn more. This could be a question, a statement, or a story.
- Get to the point quickly and explain what you do in a way that is easy to understand.
- Highlight your unique value proposition. What makes you different from your competitors? What value do you offer to your customers? I have a saying that does this for my office furniture dealership, it goes like this;

"We help organizations make their office
space a MAGNET and
NOT A MANDATE!"
This resonates with everyone in a post-Covid world.

- <u>Use strong action verbs.</u> Instead of saying "I am a sales representative," say "I help businesses increase productivity and cut expenses."
- <u>Practice</u> delivering your elevator speech until it is smooth and natural.
- <u>Have ample business cards</u>. Yes, physical business cards.

<u>Author's Note on Business Cards</u>:

I ran a LinkedIn poll, "In face-to-face, live networking events do you prefer…

- Digital Business Card?
- Physical Business Card?
- Both a Physical Business Card with QR Code on it?"

<u>Results</u>:

1. **46%** - Physical Business Card
2. **39%** - Both a Physical Business Card with QR Digital Code on it
3. **14%** - Digital Business Card

So, (based on this poll and my own experience/preference) please have physical cards and, if possible, have a scannable QR code on them to offer your digital contact information.

Therefore, having an effective elevator speech is an essential tool for any business networker. By following the tips above, you can create an elevator speech that will help you to make a positive impression on others and generate interest in you and your product or services.

<u>**Personal Example:**</u>

I cannot tell you how many times I've shown up to a networking function (admittedly sometimes a bit late) when the host has the floor with either a microphone or just with the attendee's full attention or both, and they look at me and say, "Hello there, tell us who you are and what you do." Dear reader, you need to be ready for this "in season and out of season" so you can rattle off your name, title, your business, location, and what you do or sell. If you want to get this engrained in you, visit a speed networking event where you have 2 minutes to pitch yourself and your business to the person across from you and after you each have 2 minutes to do so, you move to the next person. You will hit dozens of people in a short period of time. Therefore, after a speed Networking event like this, trust me, you will have your pitch down COLD! You can find these events at local Chambers of Commerce, they do them all the time and they do them REALLY well!

Think of your elevator speech as a brief personal and professional _brand statement_.
It is a way to communicate your unique value proposition and what you can offer to the world.
When you have a strong elevator speech you will be more confident and successful
in your networking endeavors.

Commandment 5

5. Build a Diverse Network:

Network with individuals from various industries, backgrounds, and positions. A diverse network can provide different perspectives, knowledge, and opportunities. Attend events outside your immediate field to expand your connections.

A diverse network is one that includes people from different backgrounds, industries, and roles. This type of network is important for business networkers because it provides them with access to a wider range of resources and connections.

Here are some of the <u>benefits</u> of building a diverse network:

- <u>Access to a wider range of resources</u>. When you have a diverse network, you have access to a wider range of expertise. This can be invaluable when you are facing challenges or trying to achieve new goals.
- <u>Exposure to new ideas and perspectives</u>. This can help you to think more creatively and solve problems for yourself and others more effectively.
- <u>Networking with people from different industries</u> can help you to learn about new markets and opportunities for your business. This can help you to expand your reach and grow your revenue.
- <u>Gives you the chance to build relationships</u> with potential partners and customers. This can be beneficial for your business in several ways, such

as increasing your sales and generating new leads.

Here are some <u>tips</u> for building a diverse network:
- <u>Attend diverse industry events</u>. Industry events are a great place to meet people from different backgrounds and industries. Make sure to attend a variety of events to meet a wide range of people.
- <u>Join online communities.</u> There are many online communities for business professionals. Joining these communities is a terrific way to connect with people from all over the world. Almost every social media app has groups you can join and participate in.
- <u>Reach out to people on LinkedIn</u>. LinkedIn is a great platform for networking with business professionals. Reach out to people who you find interesting and see if they would be willing to connect with you.
- <u>Be helpful and supportive</u>. The best way to build a strong network is to be helpful and supportive of others. Offer your help and advice to others, and they will be more likely to help you in return.

Building a diverse network takes time and effort, but it is worth it overall. By following these tips, you can build a diverse network that will help you to achieve your business and personal goals.

<u>Personal Example</u>:
I was invited to a Hispanic Chamber of Commerce luncheon at the Professional Business

Club I joined**, the Citrus Club in Downtown Orlando by a fellow Member who was hosting this event. Mind you, I am a mix of Italian, German, and Irish, so my only connection to Hispanic culture is my 4 years of taking conversational Spanish in High School and College. Regardless, I went and met the President and Vice President of the Hispanic Chamber of Commerce and found out it was the largest Chamber of Commerce in the Central Florida region. Because of this, I joined their Chamber and I and my sales team are actively involved and developing fruitful business connections and relationships. The influence this group has in every aspect of the Orlando and Central Florida area is immense. I would have never thought to join their Chamber had I not been willing to think a bit differently about my Networking approach and strategy.

You should think of building a diverse network as an investment in your personal brand.
When you invest in your network, you are investing in yourself and gaining marketplace credibility that enhances your personal and professional brand.
A diverse network will give you the resources and support you need to succeed in your career.

**BTW, joining a private business club where you can take people to lunch and events – invite only - would be a REALLY good idea for you to do also.

Commandment 6

6. Follow Up!

After meeting someone, try to follow up within a few days – <u>within 24 hours</u> is preferred, if possible. Send a personalized message expressing your gratitude for the conversation and mentioning something specific you discussed. Also, mention something to compliment them on. These gestures demonstrate your genuine interest and helps maintain the connection.

If the conversation went REALLY well, and you found great value in meeting this person, invite them to coffee or lunch – right away! This is where the Private Club membership comes in handy for me.

Follow-up is an essential part of networking, as it allows you to build relationships further and nurture your connections.

Here are some of the <u>benefits</u> of following up as a business networker:

- <u>Stay top of mind.</u> When you follow up with people after you have met them, you stay top of mind with your new connection. This means that they are more likely to think of you when they need your services or when they know someone who does.
- <u>Relationship-building</u>. Following up is a sure proof way to build relationships with people. It shows that you are interested in them and that you valued their time.

- <u>Nurture your connections</u>. Networking is not a one-time event. It is an ongoing process of building and maintaining relationships. Following up is a wonderful way to nurture your connections and keep them strong.
- <u>Generate leads and sales</u>. Following up can lead to new leads and sales. When you stay in touch with people, they are more likely to remember you and refer you to others.

Here are some <u>tips</u> for following up as a business networker:
- <u>Send a thank-you note</u>. After you meet someone at a Networking event, send them a thank-you note. This is an exceptional way to show your appreciation for their time and to reiterate your interest in staying in touch.
- <u>Connect with your new contacts on LinkedIn quickly</u> – like and comment on a few of their last posts as this will build trust and the currency of a "like" these days is priceless! This will allow you to stay in touch with them and see what they are up to.

    BTW, if someone "likes" your post, send them a message thanking them from time to time. It shows you are watching.
- <u>Send them relevant articles and resources</u>. If you see something that you think your new contacts would find interesting or helpful, send it to them. This shows that you are thinking of them and that you want to provide them with value.
- <u>Schedule a follow-up call or meeting</u>. Once you have established a rapport with your new

contacts, schedule a follow-up call or meeting. This is a fantastic way to get to know them better and to explore potential opportunities for collaboration.

In summary, following up is an essential part of networking. By following the tips above, you can ensure that you are following up effectively and building strong relationships with your new contacts.

Personal Example:

I recently received three different handwritten thank you cards from great connections I made at several Networking functions and one of them was from a new connection in her early 20's and the two other gentlemen were in their early 30's. IMPRESSIVE and refreshing to see!

One follow-up story I have of using a hand-written card was when I was a Shaw Hard Surface rep calling on Residential Flooring Retail Dealers. I had just met with the hard surface buyer, Tom, of a chain of flooring stores in Buffalo, NY and I was trying to get him to stock my latest laminate flooring product called "**Bullseye**." "**Bullseye**" was a natural red oak looking pattern; one color with a smoking great price if you took pallets of it. Tom was reluctant to promise me anything in my initial meeting with him. He was known to be quite standoff-ish and intimidating to us reps begging for some crumbs from his big checkbook. So, after the meeting, I sent him a hand-written thank you note and signed it "**Bullseye Bob**" with a very amateur hand-drawn target with an arrow hitting the bullseye. Well, I hit the target with this follow-up thank-you card and he called me back to tell me how much he enjoyed my card and gave me a stocking order on **"Bullseye"** laminate that was sold in all 5 of his stores. This opened up several other products I would subsequently stock with him. GOLD BABY!

I encourage you to think of follow-up to nurture your relationships and grow your network. When you follow up with people, you are showing them that you care about your relationship with them and that you are interested in their success. This will help you to build rock-solid relationships that will benefit you for years to come.

Commandment 7

7. Utilize Social Media:

Social media platforms like LinkedIn, Instagram, Twitter (now X), Tic Tok, and Facebook can be powerful tools as an extension of your networking activities.

Create a professional online presence, connect with industry professionals, join relevant groups or communities, and engage in conversations. Share valuable content and contribute your expertise to establish yourself as a trusted resource.

Social media is a powerful tool for business Networking. It allows you to connect with people from all over the world and build relationships with potential clients, partners, and mentors. It should also be a tool used as a complement to your face-to-face business development and live networking endeavors.

Personal Example:

Typically, I have multiple events I go to throughout the week. Therefore, I gather lots of photos and selfies from those events and do an end-of-the-week recap on my LinkedIn, Insta, and Facebook. In these posts, I show lots of pictures of as many people as I can from those various events and the cool part is…those posts get views, likes, shares, and comments while I'm enjoying my weekend.

Think of it as making money as you sleep. The side benefit of this is people will want you at their events and in their pictures when you show up because they know you will be posting them in your "pictorial essays" on social media. I now get people coming up to me and saying, "Can I get a picture with you?"

Be a Networking Rock Star!

Here are some of the <u>benefits</u> of utilizing social media as a business networker:

- <u>Reach a wide audience.</u> Social media allows you to reach a wide audience with your message. You can connect with people from all over the world, regardless of their industry or location.
- <u>Build relationships</u>. Social media is a great way to build relationships with people. You can share your content, engage in conversations, and provide value to your followers. This will help you to build trust and rapport with people.
- <u>Generate leads and sales</u>. Social media can lead to new leads and sales. When you share valuable content and engage with your followers, they are more likely to be interested in your products or services.

Here are some <u>tips</u> for utilizing social media as a business networker:

- <u>Create a professional profile</u>. Make sure your social media profiles are professional and reflect your brand. Use high-quality photos and videos and write clear and concise bios.
- <u>Share valuable content</u>. Share content that is relevant to your target audience and that provides them with value. This could include blog posts, articles, polls, infographics, videos, and images.

- <u>Engage with your followers</u>. Respond to comments and questions and participate in relevant conversations. This will help you to build relationships with your followers and establish yourself as an expert in your field.
- <u>Use relevant hashtags</u>. Hashtags are a great way to get your content seen by more people. Use relevant hashtags in your posts to reach people who are interested in the topics you are writing about.
- <u>Join online groups</u> (as mentioned before). There are many groups on social media for business professionals. Joining these groups is a beneficial way to connect with people from your and other related industries and learn from their experiences.

To sum up, utilizing social media is an essential part of business networking! By following the tips above, you can use social media to reach a wider audience, build relationships, generate leads and sales, and stay top of mind with your followers.

As a mindset coach, I encourage you to think of social media as a tool for connection and collaboration. When you use social media to build relationships and share valuable content, you are creating a positive impact on the world. This will help you to attract positive energy and opportunities into your life.

Commandment 8

8. Offer Value:

Networking is not just about what you can gain; it is also about what you can offer. Be proactive in helping others by sharing resources, providing advice, or making introductions. Offering value builds trust and strengthens your relationships.

Offering value is one of the most important things you can do as a business networker. When you offer value to others, you show them that you are interested in helping them achieve their personal and professional goals and that you have something to contribute. This will help you to build relationships and create a positive reputation.

Here are some of the <u>benefits</u> of offering value as a business networker:

- <u>Build value = build trust = build relationships.</u>
- <u>Offering value is a wonderful way to build relationships with people.</u> When you help others, they are more likely to want to help you in return. This leads to stronger relationships and more opportunities for collaboration.
- <u>Create a positive reputation</u>. When you offer value to others, you create a positive reputation for yourself. People will see you as a helpful and supportive person, and they will be more likely to do business with you or refer you to others.
- <u>Generate leads and sales</u>. Offering value can lead to new leads and sales. When you help people, they are more likely to be interested in your

products or services. This is because they know that you are committed to helping them succeed.

Here are some <u>tips</u> for offering value as a business networker:

- <u>Share your knowledge and expertise</u>. One of the best ways to offer value is to share your knowledge and expertise with others. You can do this by writing blog posts, giving presentations, or simply answering people's questions.
- <u>Make introductions</u>. Another way to offer value is to make introductions between people who you think could benefit from getting to know each other. This helps people build their own networks and create new opportunities for themselves. On average I do about 3-5 introductions a week and the appreciation gained from both parties is priceless in adding value.

<u>Author's Note</u>:

If I tell someone I am going to make an email introduction to one of my connections, I will do it as quickly as possible. When I do it though, I expect both parties to reply in a reasonable amount of time. Please do not be flakey and not respond to an email introduction someone makes for you. It is a big pet peeve of mine.

- <u>Offer to help with projects</u>. If you know someone who is working on a project, offer to help them. This could involve anything from providing feedback to offering to lend a hand with the work itself.

- <u>Promote other people's businesses</u>. When you see someone else sharing valuable content or promoting their business, be sure to share it with your own network. This helps support others and show them that you value what they are doing.

Consequently, you can offer value to others and reap the benefits of a strong network.

<u>Personal Example:</u>

After every meaningful conversation I have with a new connection I meet at a networking function, I try to always remember to ask,

"What can I do for you?"

These six words open the door for you to offer value to the new relationship. I met a real estate developer at a Friday morning coffee event, and I asked her this question and she responded by letting me know that she needed capital for land acquisition. I promised that I would connect her to someone on my county's Chamber of Commerce's Economic Development Committee. My fellow committee person had (and still has) a direct connection to South and Central American investors that wanted to fund land and building projects in Central Florida. They are now connected and working on several deals. BOOM, VALUE ADDED!

In summary, adding value is not only helpful to others, but also rewarding to your feeling of self-accomplishment. It's good for the world and good for your soul!

Commandment 9

9. Attend Informal Gatherings:

Networking does not always have to happen at formal events. Informal gatherings, such as meetups, happy hours, or alumni events, etc. can be excellent opportunities to connect with like-minded individuals in a more relaxed setting.

As a business coach and mentor, I believe attending informal gatherings is an essential part of being a successful business networker. Informal gatherings are events where people can come together to socialize and connect in a relaxed setting. This type of environment is ideal for networking because it allows people to get to know each other on a more personal level.

Here are some <u>benefits</u> of attending informal gatherings as a business networker:
- <u>Meet new people</u>. Informal gatherings are a great place to meet new people from different industries and backgrounds. This is a great way to expand your network and connect with people who could potentially help you achieve your business and personal goals.
- <u>Informal gatherings are another way to build relationships with people</u>. When you spend time with people in a relaxed setting, you are more likely to get to know them on a personal level and build trust.
- <u>Learn about new opportunities</u>. You may meet people who are working on new projects or who

have information about new trends in your industry or marketplace.

- <u>Get referrals</u>. Informal gatherings are a great place to get referrals. When people know you on a personal level, they are more likely to refer you to their friends and colleagues.

Here are some <u>tips</u> for Networking at informal gatherings:

- <u>Be yourself</u>. People can tell when you are being fake, so it is important to be yourself and let your personality shine through.
- <u>Be helpful</u>. Offer to help others with their drinks, snacks, or anything else they may need. This makes a good impression and show that you are a team player.
- <u>Follow up.</u> Goes without saying.☺

In conclusion, attending informal gatherings expands your network, builds relationships, exposes you to new opportunities, and gets you that referral. With these simple steps you can make the most of your time at informal gatherings and achieve your Networking goals.

<u>Personal Example:</u>

Happy Hours or Business After-Hours events are much less formal and are some of the best Networking opportunities because everyone lets their guard down and they are much more open, laid-back…and approachable. We started hosting these types of "After Hours" at our Club and they have exploded in attendance. Starting with young executives/professionals and all the mature executives and professions just started showing up, so we had to change the name. This started at around 30 attendees and within a few months is now drawing in about 130!

But the point is, people crave this type of setting, especially if there is light entertainment and light food. Invite fellow networkers to these informal events. Chambers of Commerce's LOVE to do these and I have met and stayed connected with countless people because of going to these type of informal networking gatherings.

As a business mentor coach, I encourage you to think of attending informal gatherings as an opportunity to gain experience and grow. Don't be afraid to step outside of your comfort zone and meet new people.

You never know who you might meet or what opportunities might come your way.

Commandment 10

10. Maintain Relationships:

Networking is an ongoing process. Stay in touch with your connections by periodically reaching out, sharing interesting articles or opportunities, or meeting for coffee. Nurture your relationships to ensure they remain strong and mutually beneficial.

As a networking veteran, yet always a student of the "craft", I believe that maintaining relationships is one of the most important things you can do as a business networker. Relationships are the foundation of any successful business network. When you have strong relationships with people, they are more likely to trust you, refer you to others, and help you achieve your business goals.

Many business scholars and professional marketers have said that every month a contact does not hear from you, they forget about you 10%! So after five months of them not hearing or seeing you, they've forgotten about you 50%. WOW!

Here are some of the <u>benefits</u> of maintaining relationships as a business networker:

- <u>Build trust</u>. Trust is essential for any successful relationship. When people trust you, they are more likely to do business with you and refer you to others.
- <u>Generate sales and income</u>. The stronger your relationships are with people, the more likely they are to refer you to their friends and

colleagues. This can lead to new leads and sales opportunities for your business.

- <u>Get support</u>. When you have strong relationships with other business professionals, you have a network of people who can support you and help you overcome challenges and achieve your personal and professional goals.

Here are some <u>tips</u> for maintaining relationships as a business networker:

- <u>Stay in touch</u>. Try to stay in touch with your network contacts on a regular basis. You can do this by sending them emails, direct messages on social media sites, connecting with them on social media, or scheduling coffee meetings or lunches.

The Guru of Networking, Keith Farrazi, in the networking classic *Never Eat Alone* suggests…

"Ping constantly:
*It's important to reach out to those in your circle of contacts all the time –
not just when you need something."*

Keith Ferrazzi and Tahl Raz, *"Never Eat Alone and Other Secrets To Success, One Relationship At A Time."* 2005, Crown Publishing Group, sleeve of front cover.

- <u>Remember this? Provide value.</u> Look for ways to provide value to your network contacts. This could involve sharing helpful content, referring them to other businesses, or offering to help them with their projects.
- <u>Be supportive</u>. Be there for your network contacts when they need you. This could involve offering advice, connecting them with other

people, or simply being a sounding board. Also, support any events they are hosting or inviting you to. This will go a L O N G way!

Maintaining relationships is essential for any successful business networker. By following these tips you can nurture your relationships and build a strong network that will help you achieve your business goals.

<u>Personal Example</u>:
I strive to collect the business cards I gather from meaningful (and not so meaningful) conversations at the various networking events I attend. I have someone enter the basic contact information off those cards into a spreadsheet and then I upload them to CRM. I now send out frequent newsletters to that ever-growing list as well as invites to events I am hosting or going to.
My network loves this and they are grateful they are in the loop of where the hottest new meet-up is going to be.

Always be a networking resource, it pays priceless dividends!

In summary, maintaining relationships can be viewed as a way to invest in your future. When you invest in your relationships, you are investing in yourself and your future. A strong network will give you the support and resources you need to succeed in your career, business, and personal life.

Mini-Wrap Up/Conclusion

To keep this book mini, here is a short wrap-up:

Remember, networking is all about
building genuine relationships,
so be authentic, respectful, and patient.
It takes time and consistent effort to develop trust
and therefore to develop a robust network,
but the rewards can be significant.
Re-read these 10 Commandments
and you will succeed in Networking.
Guaranteed!

**Best Wishes in Your Networking Mastery!
You've Got This!**

Please shoot me an email to let me know how you
liked this mini-book and how it helped you.
Also, please share success stories. God Bless!

Rb3solutions@outlook.com

➢ To track my current and on-going Networking activities and "nuggets of truth" follow me on my LinkedIn page at…
https://www.linkedin.com/in/robertbagley3rd

➢ View my Professional Profile Website at…
http://robertbagley3rd.com

➢ To enjoy a Podcast where I discuss my experiences and dive more into networking strategies, please visit this interview of me with Luminary Panel hosts, Chonsten Jennings and Lilliana Fedewa at…

"How To Overcome Setbacks to Keep Succeeding No Matter What!"
https://youtu.be/x2vjb-yTon8?si=ajWFD_G0EMiuJ52o

➢ To see my other "mini-books" and published work, please visit my Author Page at…
https://amazon.com/author/rb3